Properties of Materials

Hard or Soft

Charlotte Guillain

www.raintreepublishers.co.uk
Visit our website to find out
more information about
Raintree books.

To order:
☎ Phone 0845 6044371
▤ Fax +44 (0) 1865 312263
▧ Email myorders@capstonepub.co.uk

Customers from outside the UK please telephone +44 1865 312262

Raintree is an imprint of Capstone Global Library Limited,
a company incorporated in England and Wales having its
registered office at 7 Pilgrim Street, London, EC4V 6LB
– Registered company number: 6695582

Edited by Charlotte Guillain and Catherine Veitch
Designed by Joanna Hinton-Malivoire
Picture research by Elizabeth Alexander
Originated by Heinemann Library
Printed by South China Printing Company Limited

ISBN 978 0 431 19345 8 (hardback)
13 12 11 10 09
10 9 8 7 6 5 4 3 2 1

ISBN 978 0 431 19353 3 (paperback)
14 13 12 11 10
10 9 8 7 6 5 4 3 2 1

British Library Cataloguing in Publication Data
Guillain, Charlotte
Hard or soft. – (Properties of materials)
530.4
A full catalogue record for this book is available from the British
Library.

Acknowledgements
The author and publishers are grateful to the following for
permission to reproduce copyright material:
Alamy pp. **6** (© Geoff du Feu), **10** (© Dirk V. Mallinckrodt);
© Capstone Publishers pp. **8**, **19**, **22** (Karon Dubke); © Corbis
p. **15**; Corbis pp. **20** (© Image Source), **21**, **23** middle
(© Graham Bell); Getty Images p. **14** (Somos/Veer); Photolibrary
pp. **13** (Stockdisc/Stockbyte), **18** (Imagesource); Shutterstock
pp. **4** (© Gilmanshin), **5** (© Ilja Mašík), **7** (© Leonid Katsyka),
9 (© Mindy W. M. Chung), **11**, **23** bottom (© GoodMood
Photo), **12**, **23** top (© Olivier Le Queinec), **16** (© PhotoSky.4t.
com), **17** (© IKO).

Cover photograph of the Devil's Marbles reproduced with
permission of © Dorling Kindersley (Alan Keohane). Back cover
photograph of a girl knocking on a door reproduced with permission
of Photolibrary (Imagesource).

The publishers would like to thank Nancy Harris and Adriana
Scalise for their assistance in the preparation of this book.

Every effort has been made to contact copyright holders
of any material reproduced in this book. Any omissions
will be rectified in subsequent printings if notice is given to the
publisher.

Contents

Hard materials

Some things are hard.

It is not easy to change the shape of hard things.

Hard things can be heavy.

Hard things can be strong.

Soft materials

Some things are soft.

It is easy to change the shape of soft things.

Soft things can be light.

Soft things can be stretchy.

Hard and soft materials

Metal is hard.

Metal can be strong.

Wool is soft.

Wool can be stretchy.

Glass is hard.

Glass can be heavy.

Cotton is soft.

Cotton can be light.

Rock is hard. It is not easy to change the shape of rock.

Clay is soft. It is easy to change the shape of wet clay.

You can feel if something is hard.

You can feel if something is soft.

Hard things are not easy to squeeze.

Soft things are easy to squeeze.

Quiz

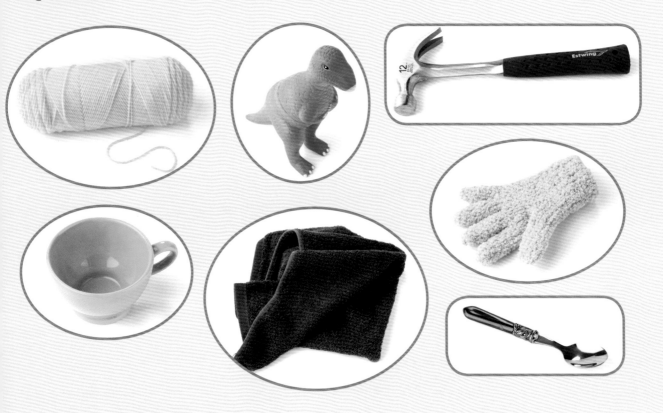

Which of these things are hard?
Which of these things are soft?

Picture glossary

metal hard, shiny material

squeeze press something tightly

stretchy something that can get
longer or wider, especially by pulling

Index

Note to parents and teachers
Before reading
Tell children materials can be hard or soft. Materials that are hard can be heavy and cannot change shape easily. Materials that are soft can be light, easy to squeeze, and can change shape easily. Hold up different types of pictures of soft and hard materials. Ask children to describe the pictures. Ask if the objects are hard or soft.

After reading
Discuss with children the different types of materials they saw in the book. Ask children: "What did you notice about the hard and soft materials?", "If you were to build a house, what materials would you want your house to be made out of?". Read a traditional version of *The Three Little Pigs*, and ask children to think about what type of material built the strongest house for the pigs. After reading, ask children to work in small groups to investigate various building materials (polystyrene, toothpicks, clay, Lego blocks, paper, cardboard, etc). Tell children to divide their materials into two groups, hard and soft. Ask them which group of materials is better to build a house and why. After the discussion, let children work in groups to build their own houses, then discuss which ones are the strongest.